COLORS FOR LIFE
Coloring Book

Angela González
Illustration, design and texts

For Alicia, Tomás, Martín, María del Mar and Elisa my little big loves

Angela González, Lala, was born in Medellín, Colombia. Since she
was little she remembers having a very particular taste for drawing and illustration.
Lala studie Graphic Design and then drawing and oil painting.
Lala´s talent and perseverance have enabled her to work in the fields of illustration
and art, where she has captured a colorful, magical, and Naïve art movement style,
playing with her images to represent the most beautiful scenes of her own fairytales.
Colombia has always been Lala´s source of inspiration, its culture, folklore, landscapes
and flowers are reflected in her work, a country that is definitely for her a wonderland.

Copyright 2016 © Original title: Colores para la vida
All Rights Reserved
Illustrations, design and text: Angela González
Translation: Maria Marcela González Toro
www.lalagonzalez.com
Instagram: @lalagonzalezartista
ISBN: 978-958-48-6438-3
Created in Colombia, Printed in USA

No part of this publication may be reproduced, distributed, or transmited
in any form or by any means, including photocopying, or other electronic
or mechanical methods, without the prior written permission of the owner
of intellectual property.

One thousand smiles trapped, just one opens my heart

I tell my own wonderful stories, I color my own blue sky

I catch ilusions in the sea of happiness

At night I close my eyes and I see the light that lights up my heart

I want to fill my heart in a sea of sweet memories

The charm of a princess who believes in love

I see you with the eyes of my heart and feel with my soul

Tips:

- Preferably use colored pencils, markers work better when drawing small details and decorating with dots and lines.

- Place a sheet of cardstock behind the page you are going to color, allowing high lighting the colors and making pressure for well diffused areas.

- Chose a quiet space

- Good ilumination

- Take breakes and exercise your hands

Coloring takes you to a wonderful stage of calm and serenity, a magical gift for your soul.

ENJOY, LEARN AND BE HAPPY